How Much Is a Little Boy Worth?

Rachael and Jacob Denhollander

Illustrated by Marcin Piwowarski

Tyndale House Publishers
Carol Stream, Illinois

Visit Tyndale's website for kids at tyndale.com/kids.

Tyndale is a registered trademark of Tyndale House Ministries. The Tyndale Kids logo is a trademark of Tyndale House Ministries.

How Much Is a Little Boy Worth?

Designed by Jacqueline L. Nuñez

Edited by Sarah Rubio

Published in association with the literary agency of United Talent Agency, LLC, 888 Seventh Avenue, 7th Floor, New York, New York 10106, USA.

For manufacturing information regarding this product, please call 1-855-277-9400.

For information about special discounts for bulk purchases, please contact Tyndale House Publishers at csresponse@tyndale .com, or call 1-855-277-9400.

Library of Congress Cataloging-in-Publication Data

A catalog record for this book is available from the Library of Congress.

ISBN 978-1-4964-5483-6

Printed in China

28	27	26	25	24	23
7	6	5	4	3	2

Letter to Readers

The titular question of this book is one that every boy and every man will answer. They may never realize that they have answered this question, but eventually, the hundreds of messages they receive over their lifetimes will coalesce to form a core part of their identity. How a young boy answers the question "How much is a little boy worth?" will shape the sort of man he grows into and the way he learns to value not only himself but those all around him.

As we watch our own young son and his friends, we wonder, "What messages are they hearing now?" In their own play and in their interactions with adults, they are constantly casting out feelers, trying to figure out where they fit into everything: "Dad, do you like my LEGO car?" "Mom, did I do a good job?" The sideways glances as they share their favorite song or movie, hoping it meets the approval of their friends. Little boys want to know that they are good enough, that they have met the standard for approval. We have seen the devastation in their eyes when they perceive themselves as failures, outcasts, or damaged. It is not merely disappointment at having failed to achieve a goal or an outcome; it is confusion about their worth: *Why am I so stupid? Why does no one like me? Why can't I just be better?*

There are many voices competing to tell our boys what they are worth, and most of them point to external standards—what they can do, what they wear, who they know, how fast they can run, how many friends they have. Our boys can easily live dependent on the opinions of others or view themselves through the lens of trauma they have endured or evaluate themselves in light of mistakes they have made. We believe one of the most important things every adult can do for the little boys in their lives is to confront these harmful messages by whispering the truth over and over and over again to them.

Our boys need to know that their worth is not derived from or dependent on external sources. It comes from how they were made, and by whom. Our boys need to know that their value is intrinsic to who they are, not based on what they can do or what others have done to them. Our boys need to know whose voice to listen to and how to measure their value. This frees them from the social pressures that can threaten every facet of who they are; it frees them to heal when they have suffered; and it frees them to stand for what is right, no matter what anyone says.

In the rare moments when he is still, we like to take our son in our arms to make sure he knows how much we love him. Not because everything he does is perfect, but because he is of inestimable worth. Because he is an incredible creature, created by an incredible Creator. It's our hope that as you read this book with your little boy, his heart will be filled with this awesome truth. That he will be able to see the vastness and power of creation and know that he has value beyond even the stars. That he will feel deep in his soul that his value is not found in what he accomplishes or what anyone else says. That he will know he is of incalculable worth because he is made in the image of God. And we pray that grown-ups will also receive this message, which, after all, is the answer to the question everyone asks: "What am I worth?" The answer, dear soul, is "everything."

With much love for every little boy, grown and small, who needs to know how much he is worth,

Rachael & Jacob

How much, how much, are you worth, precious boy?

How much is a little boy worth?

More than the stars and the moon in the sky,
More than the sun up above,

More than all the incredible things in this world,
It is you that I treasure and love.

Fearfully and wonderfully made to be loved,
Valuable just 'cause you're you.
Uniquely designed, you are one of a kind.
Little boy, do you know this is true?

6

Your body and mind, your heart and your soul,
Were all made in His image, made to be whole.

You are worth speaking up for, worth any fight,
Worth all the cost of choosing what's right.
Worth sacrifices, worth doing hard things,
Worth standing beside you, whatever life brings.

Worth more than winning or power or gold,

Worth whatever it takes for your worth to be told.

Worth raising my voice to shout what is true,
Worth holding you close to say, "I love you."

Worth trying again, worth working hard,

Worth being with you, playing tag in the yard.

Worth standing up tall, worth standing alone,
Worth bearing the cost for the truth to be known.

How much, how much are you worth, precious boy?

How much is a little boy worth?

More than the stars and the moon in the sky,

More than the sun up above,

More than all the incredible things in this world,

It is you that I treasure and love.

Your worth doesn't come from being in charge,
Or from money or fame to be won.
Your value is found in how you were made—
Worth everything, even God's Son.

Your worth doesn't change; it can never be lost.

It won't melt away like a cold winter frost.

No matter what happens, your worth will remain.

At the end of the day, it will stay just the same.

God is the strongest; what He says is true.

And He's told the world just how much He loves you.

He showed your value by giving His life,

Showed you are worth such a great sacrifice.

How much, how much, are you worth, precious boy?

How much is a little boy worth?

Worth infinitely more than you can imagine,

And no one can change what's been spoken by heaven.

To our "gift from God," Jonathan:

May you always know your true value and boldly live

in the knowledge that you are deeply loved.